WEEDER'S DIGEST

Joel Rothman

ЯR
RAVETTE PUBLISHING

First Published by
Ravette Publishing Limited 1997

Cartoons by Peter Dredge

Printed and bound for
Ravette Publishing Limited,
Unit 3, Tristar Centre
Star Road, Partridge Green
West Sussex RH13 8RA

by Proost, Belgium

ISBN: 1 85304 934 4

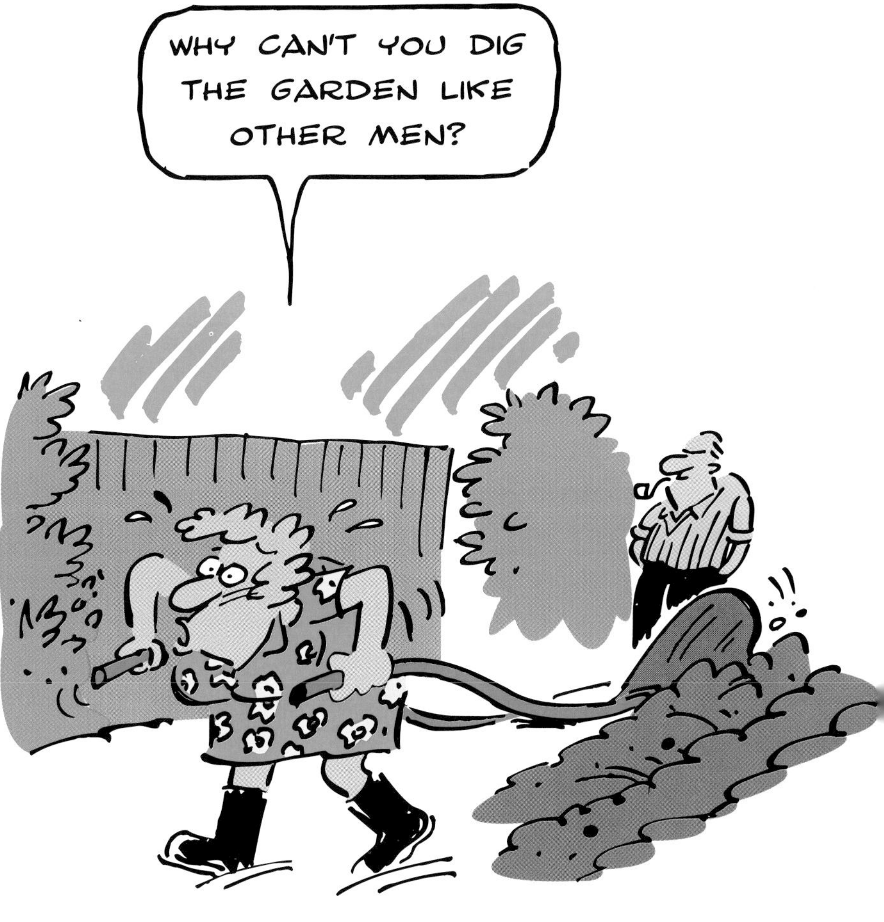
WHY CAN'T YOU DIG THE GARDEN LIKE OTHER MEN?

GRASS: SOMETHING THAT GROWS
BY INCHES AND DIES BY FEET.

MOWING THE LAWN CAN BE HARD WORK - ESPECIALLY WHEN YOU HAVE TO CONVINCE YOUR WIFE TO DO IT!

GARDENER: A PERSON WITH A SENSE OF HUMUS.

ORGANIC GARDENERS: PEOPLE WHO TILL IT LIKE IT IS.

OLD GARDENERS NEVER DIE, THEY JUST SPADE AWAY.

THE SECRET OF GARDENING SUCCESS IS TROWEL AND ERROR.

YOUR GARDEN LOOKS SO LOVELY. WHAT'S THE SECRET OF YOUR GREEN FINGERS?
AN ACHING BACK!

GARDEN: SOMETHING THAT DIES
IF YOU DON'T WATER IT AND
ROTS IF YOU DO.

AMATEUR GARDENERS: PEOPLE
WHO ARE SOMETIMES VICTIMS OF
VICIOUS PLOTS.

I KNOW ONE GARDENER WHO
GETS A KICK OUT OF TALKING
DIRTY TO PLANTS.
LAST WEEK HE WAS ARRESTED
FOR MAKING
OBSCENE FERN CALLS.

SAY IT WITH FLOWERS — GIVE
HER A TRIFFID.

WHEN MY HUSBAND SAYS IT WITH FLOWERS THE FIRST THING I SMELL IS A RAT!

I'VE LEARNED THE FIRST THING TO DO WITH A GARDEN IS TO TURN OVER THE SOIL . . . TO A GARDENER!

SUCH A THOUGHTFUL KID, WHEN
HE SAW THE SIGN "KEEP OFF THE
GRASS" HE WALKED THROUGH
THE FLOWER BED.

WHAT DID YOUR HUSBAND RAISE IN THE GARDEN THIS YEAR, MAVIS?
ONLY HIS TEMPER!

41

AUTUMN: WHEN MOTHER
NATURE GOES THROUGH A
CHANGE OF LEAF.

49

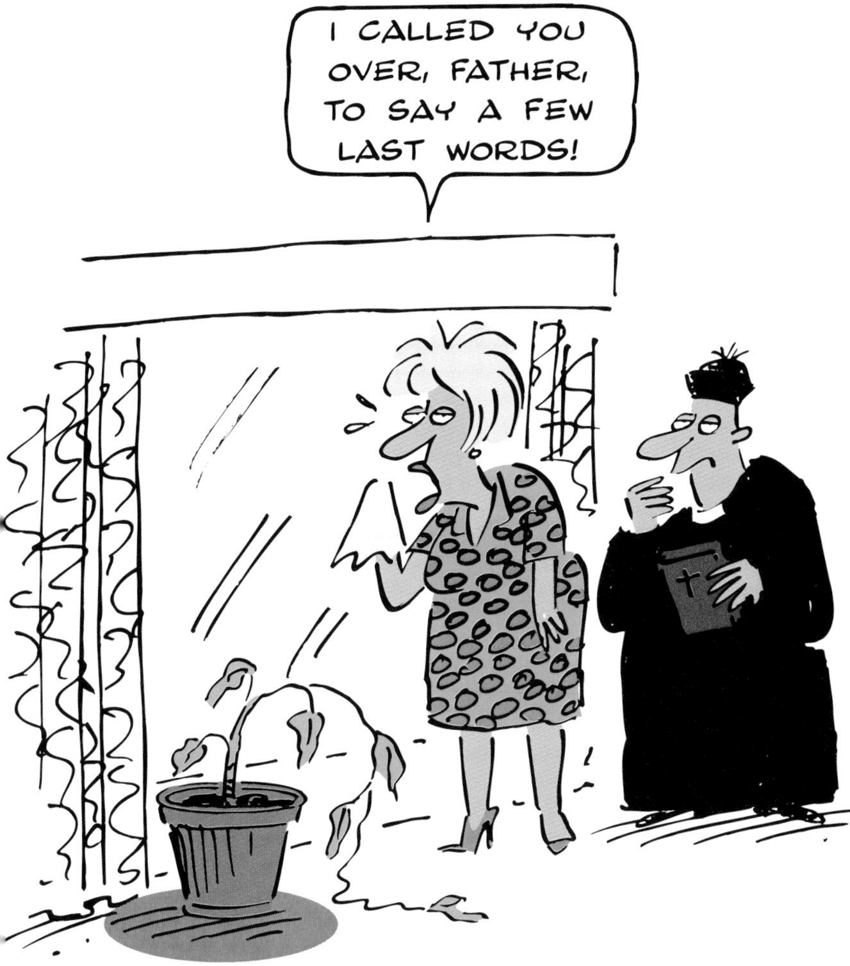
I CALLED YOU OVER, FATHER, TO SAY A FEW LAST WORDS!

IT'S GOT TWO BEDROOMS AND A KITCHEN, DEAR - THE GARDEN COULD BE A PROBLEM THOUGH!
SOLD

MR GREENE WAS DIGGING A HOLE IN HIS GARDEN WHEN SUDDENLY THE HEAD OF MR COOP APPEARED OVER THE FENCE. "WHAT ARE YOU BURYING IN THAT HOLE?" ASKED MR COOP SHARPLY. "I'M JUST REPLANTING SOME OF MY SEEDS, THAT'S ALL," WAS GREENE'S REPLY. "SEEDS! IT LOOKS MORE LIKE ONE OF MY HENS!" SAID COOP SUSPICIOUSLY. "THAT'S RIGHT," AFFIRMED GREENE, THE SEEDS ARE INSIDE.

YOU SHOULD KNOW BETTER THAN TO NAG DAD WHEN HE'S WATERING THE GARDEN!

...AND ANOTHER THING... THAT SUBSCRIPTION TO BETTER GARDENING IS RIDICULOUS!